Kids' Magical
MANDALAS

STERLING CHILDREN'S BOOKS

New York

Children and Mandalas

We often forget that children need a way to relieve stress, too. Coloring mandalas is the perfect way to help them relax and focus, while also fostering a love of art.

A mandala is a repetitive design within a circle. It can be a tool for meditation, therapy, or simply an activity to while away the time. Through their free-flowing arrangements, mandalas have a calming effect upon even the most rambunctious child. And after the mandala is completed, the finished work becomes an instrument for further reflection. It's an ideal way to combine a love of coloring with some much-needed quiet time in our hectic world.

STERLING CHILDREN'S BOOKS
New York

An Imprint of Sterling Publishing
387 Park Avenue South
New York, NY 10016

STERLING CHILDREN'S BOOKS and the distinctive Sterling Children's Books logo are trademarks of Sterling Publishing Co., Inc.

Copyright © 2003 by Edition Bücherbär im Arena Verlag GmbH, Würzburg
Introduction Copyright © 2004 by Sterling Publishing Co., Inc.
Illustrations by Rudi Moser

Published in 2004 by Sterling Publishing Co., Inc.

Originally published in Germany under the title Mandalas:
Malen und Entspannen Vorschule by
Edition Bücherbär im Arena Verlag GmbH, Würzburg
Rottendorfer Strasse 16, 97074 Würzburg, Germany

All rights reserved. No part of this publication may be reproduced, stored in a retrieval system, or transmitted, in any form or by any means, electronic, mechanical, photocopying, recording, or otherwise, without prior written permission from the publisher.

ISBN 978-1-4027-1721-5

Library of Congress Cataloging-in-Publication Data Available

Distributed in Canada by Sterling Publishing
C/o Canadian Manda Group, 165 Dufferin Street
Toronto, Ontario, Canada M6K 3H6
Distributed in the United Kingdom by GMC Distribution Services
Castle Place, 166 High Street, Lewes, East Sussex, England BN7 1XU
Distributed in Australia by Capricorn Link (Australia) Pty. Ltd.
P.O. Box 704, Windsor, NSW 2756, Australia

For information about custom editions, special sales, and premium and corporate purchases, please contact Sterling Special Sales at 800-805-5489 or specialsales@sterlingpublishing.com.

Manufactured in Canada
Lot #:
15 17 19 20 18 16 14
11/15

www.sterlingpublishing.com/kids

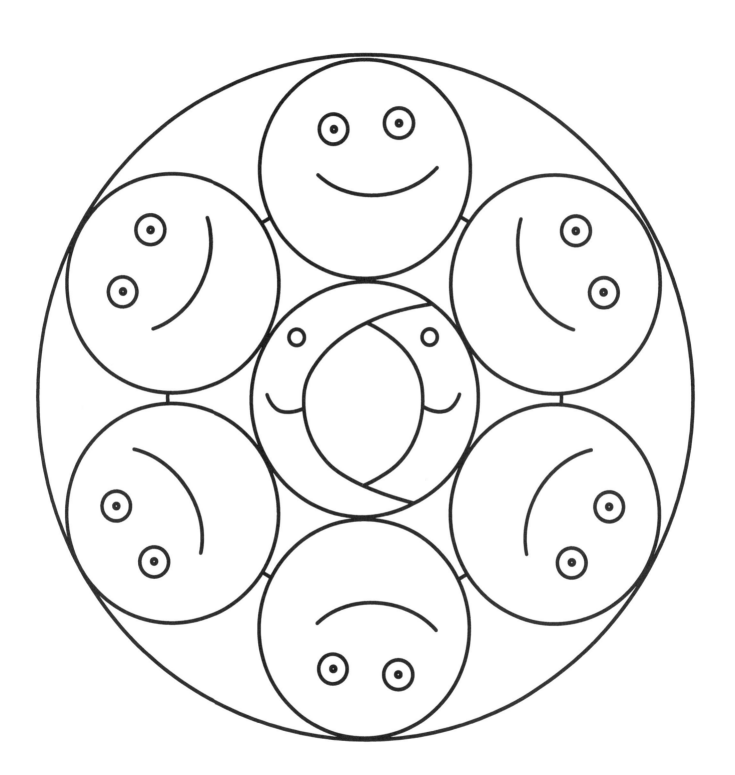

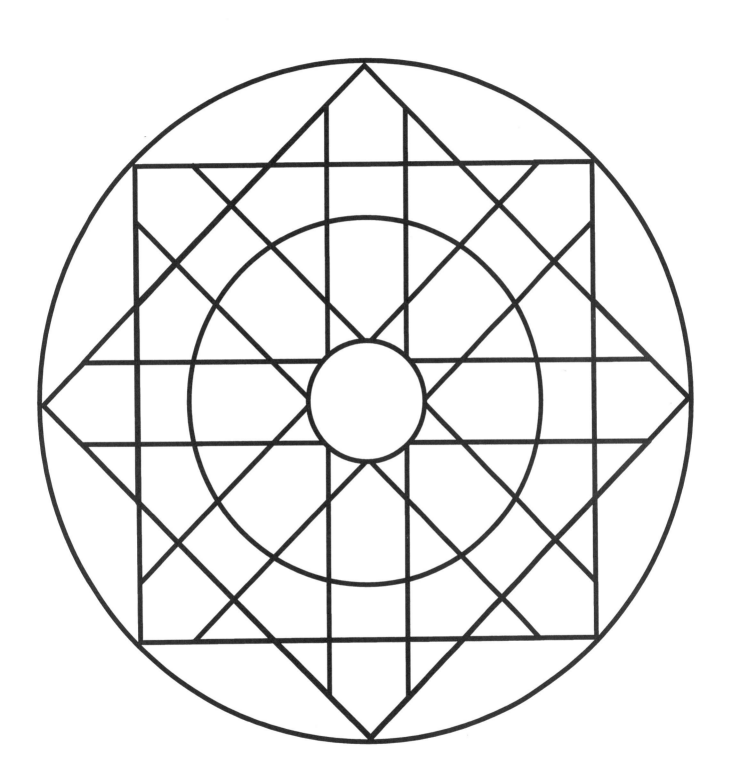

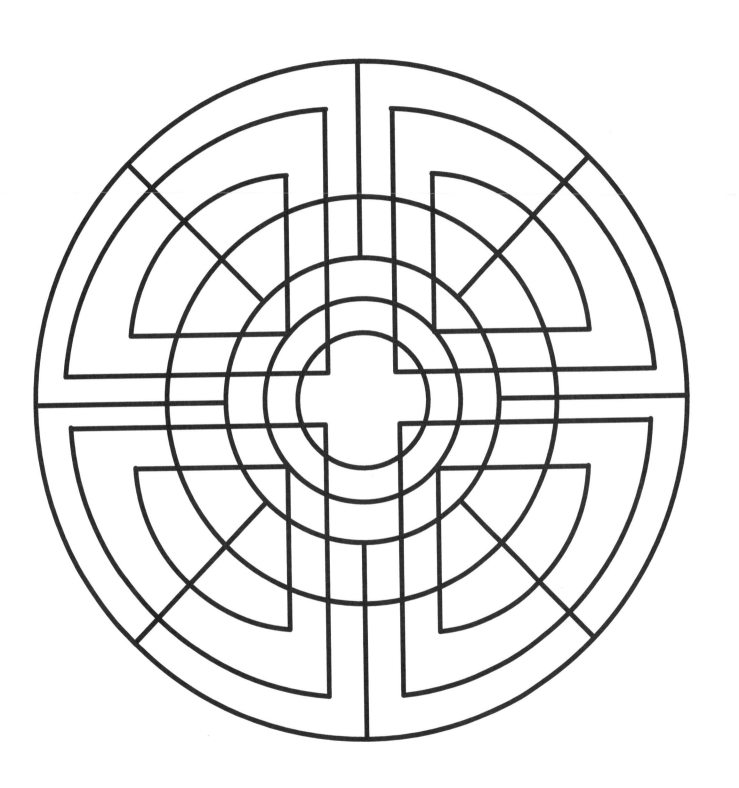

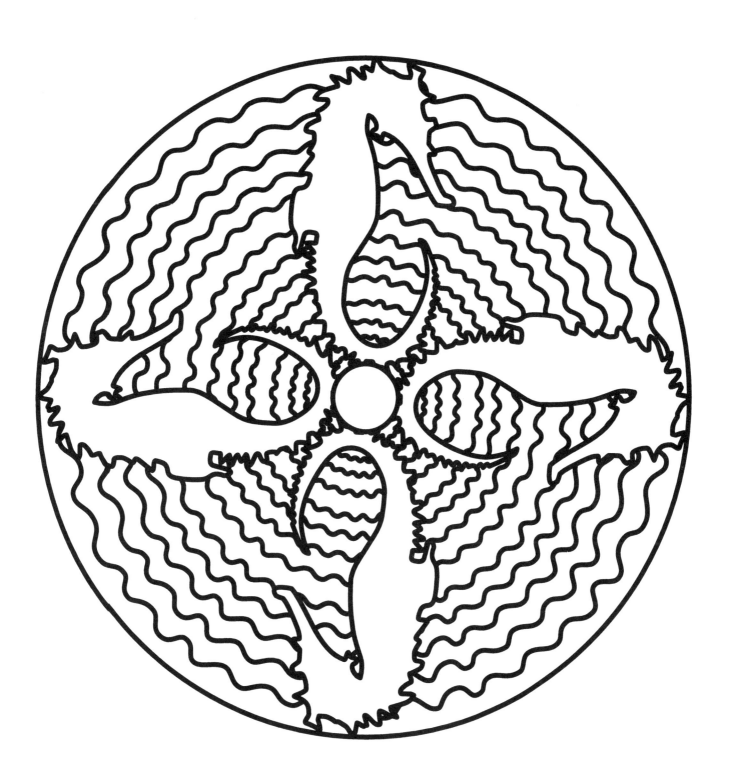

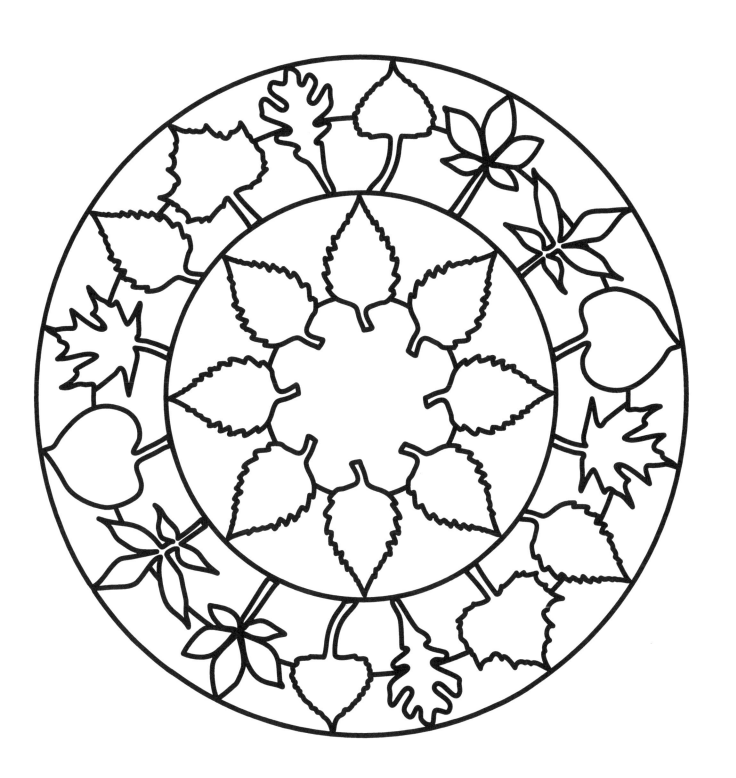